MY DEVOTION

Also by Clayton Eshleman

Poetry

Mexico & North (1962)
Indiana (1969)
Altars (1971)
Coils (1973)
The Gull Wall (1975)
What She Means (1978)
Hades in Manganese (1981)
Fracture (1983)
The Name Encanyoned River: Selected Poems 1960–1985 (1986)
Hotel Cro-Magnon (1989)
Under World Arrest (1994)
From Scratch (1998)

Prose

Antiphonal Swing: Selected Prose 1960–1985 (1986)
Companion Spider: Essays (2001)
*Juniper Fuse: Upper Paleolithic Imagination
    & the Construction of the Underworld* (2003)

Translations

Pablo Neruda, *Residence on Earth* (1962)
César Vallejo, *The Complete Posthumous Poetry*
    (with José Rubia Barcia, 1978)
Aimé Césaire, *The Collected Poetry* (with Annette Smith, 1983)
Michel Deguy, *Giving Given* (1984)
Bernard Bador, *Sea Urchin Harakiri* (1986)
*Conductors of the Pit: Major Works by Rimbaud, Vallejo, Césaire,
    Artaud & Holan* (1988)
Aimé Césaire, *Lyric & Narrative Poetry 1946–1982*
    (with Annette Smith, 1990)
César Vallejo, *Trilce* (1992, 2000)
Antonin Artaud, *Watchfiends & Rack Screams*
    (with Bernard Bador, 1995)
Aimé Césaire, *Notebook of a Return to the Native Land*
    (with Annette Smith, 2001)

Journals and anthologies

Folio (Bloomington, Indiana, 3 issues, 1959–1960)
Quena (Lima, Peru, 1 issue, edited, then suppressed
    by the North American Peruvian Cultural Institute, 1966)
Caterpillar (New York–Los Angeles, 20 issues, 1967–1973)
A Caterpillar Anthology (1971)
Sulfur (Pasadena–Los Angeles–Ypsilanti, 46 issues, 1981–2000)

CLAYTON ESHLEMAN

MY DEVOTION

A Black Sparrow Book

David R. Godine · *Publisher* · *Boston*

This is
A Black Sparrow Book
published in 2004 by
DAVID R. GODINE · *Publisher*
Post Office Box 450
Jaffrey, New Hampshire 03452
www.blacksparrowbooks.com

Certain of these poems first appeared, sometimes in different form, in the
following periodicals and Webzines: *Boston Review, Boxkite* (Australia), *Brooklyn
Rail, Columbia Poetry Review, cosmoetica* (Web site), *Denver Quarterly, Facture,
5 Trope* (Web site), *Grand Street* (Web site), *hemorrhagingimaging, House
Organ, Hunger, Milk* (Web site), *Minutes of the Charles Olson Society, Samizdat,
Skanky Possum, Smartish Pace, sourceS* (France), and *Ur Vox*.

   "Erratics" was first published, in slightly different form, as the book *Erratics*
(Hunger Press, 2001).

   "Sweetheart" was first published as a booklet for Caryl Eshleman's sixtieth
birthday (April 28, 2002) by Canopic Press.

   "Animals Out of the Snow" was selected by Robert Creeley for *The Best
American Poetry 2002* (Scribners).

Book design and composition by Carl W. Scarbrough

The Black Sparrow Books pressmark is by Julian Waters
www.waterslettering.com

Black Sparrow Books are printed on acid-free paper

Library of Congress Cataloging-in-Publication Data is available.

ISBN 1-57423-192-8

FIRST EDITION
Printed in Canada

dearest Caryl,   we are still crossing
a single-lane bridge over the Vézère River,
            over Atlementheneira, into the beyond

        trying to decipher the oldest
    yet vitally present, terribly fragmentary
        paradise of all.

CONTENTS

I

II

III

IV

V

What you wrote about *Trilce* fascinates me: "destabilized syntax operating in a relatively stable field (it is not language poetry nor is it coherent narrative)." I can only try to imagine the translation issues here. But don't you think that, in American poetry at large, the interesting work involves "destablilized syntax" and "relatively stable field"? I'm trying to imagine a poetics of absolute resistance which has critical resistance as its stable field yet can invoke many kinds of bending of language, certainly of the king's English, but which does not depend, for its testimony of resistance, simply on bending the language. . . a poetics that would be, both in spirit and in method, resistant to the calculated destabilizations of content and context in our time—hence "absolute"—neither "message of dissent" clothed in conventional format nor limited to so-called "experimental" or "medium-as-message" format—but something else: language proceeding from an indignant, outraged, undomesticated consciousness that is torqued and fired so that it indents that consciousness indelibly into the page.

—Adrienne Rich, August 1999

I

BEFORE THE WALL

Unless you attack what is wrong, in you, and in your world,
I say you repress. If you go for the throat of your moon,
you might clear a midnight of bloodspattered road.
Do we actually stand before the wall for poetry?
I can drink myself to death
but such only feels up Dionysus.
I keep saying to Nora Jaffe's soul: it is enough
to have space to write in, time, and someone to live with
who loves me, and whom I love, as if outward ceremony
    can be sloughed—
it can, and it can't. As we get older
Lorca is before the wall every morning,
Dalí is jerking him off as he dies.
Life is obscene, not because of Dalí's fist,
but because of our ability to live with eros conjunct with
    violence—
and we never know if this is fixed in limbo by fettered Titans,
if, in attempting to say the very thing we are,
we say just one self, or many, or merely register abyssal
    shudderings.
The E on the stone? Maybe it meant mountain or gate, in what way
was it turned? A two-stalled stable? Man rejoicing?
Or is this energy mounted off impotence?
Possible. A despair so clear and pure it runs through primality.

ROCK AND ROOTSTOCK

Originally, poetry is
a binding of wild to mine, a sewing of the unbound
   animal to
slowly-being-bound-person,   hybrid rock,
rock with my teeth at its core,
or my machine-gun, or my greenhouse,
erratic celestial floor—
        and to be rock is to be
the most ambivalent thing,   Ulro in Blake,
deadened deadness,   corpse breccia,   and the truth.

The speakable carbuncle of life offers some satisfaction,
it's a viceroy moment,   to imagine what one wants to exist,
but there is so much we feel around us we do not focus,
so much that affects, infests the pivot,
and what is the pivot? An amalgam, quartered by
   my desire to be
here and elope with imagination,
     to sink into its rootstock,   to be inside the moral
whose circumference is hatred,
to follow out my coal bin,
                and futurity?
On one level I'm damaged beyond Indiana recognition,
on another, I'm the phoenix a poet must be,
a ruined worker in the hive of irregularity,
of a forge so random it is mad to hammer.

FIVE QUEASY PIECES

I want to come to terms with my vaulted
and faulty
interior, with the clocks stacked in my kidneys,
with my face of a radish
draining tears into a tile sea.
And I do not want to come to terms with this vaunted
faculty, with these mer and men maids
calving right below consciousness.
Fuse and refusal,
torque of the Vallejo legacy.
To mince the baby wind—
to feast on nothing.

When I was a woman
I smiled, the arrows bristling from my face,
an old-fashioned woman, a rooted flow.
Then I became a winged pilgrim, intestinal offerings
bumping along the ground as I flew.
My ambivalence worked my negations on looms.
Now I am gutless,
peristaltic in ascent,
radiant with memories of menstrual wastes.

Sitting under this outcropping, thinking at
the speed of limestone, I hear waiters below
struggling with diners, diners sparring with food,
a breeze sweeps up the sound of gardeners
locked in combat with shoots, swimmers intercleaved
with the spermatic flex of yesterday's wind.
A workman shears the earth's head, revealing
its timed skull, limestone time, openly dead,

not closed like we are, fighting with
everything we touch, trying to become headless crosses,
gods below the horizon, gods of the mystical hollow earth.

The reason you came here
has dropped away. You have butter on your fly.
You write because your beanstalk is raced by giant Jacks.
Because the midden strata at Laugerie Haute
strikes you as the origin of fashion.
At best, a zipper meshes dualities,
the zipper of the mind interlocking its own bite.
How moving it is to hear someone say
something veined with
reflective and suffered pleasure.

Awake as if drunk with the last dream,
ready to remake whatever
—my life, my vision, my love—
to see through is to have nothing to resist,
is to lose the resistance for which one secretly lives.
Poetry from the beginning is posited,
based, on resistance,   is a work *against*,
whether with flint or quill
it is to convert one's boring into a lateral spell,
an ecstatic wandering in which one lives
as if weightless on the hunch of a finger tip—
hunchwork   wondrous release of the body
poised on the burin of itself.

CONCERNING GNOMES AND TROLLS

"On the sight of an American uniform a horde of gnomes and trolls seems to appear like magic, pouring out of doorways, as if shot from a cannon. Some hop on crutches. Some hobble on stumps of feet. Some run with angular movements. Some glide like Oriental genies. Almost all wear striped convict suits, covered with patches, or gray-black remnants of Eastern clothing."

So the half-human creatures of childhood fancy, of adult imaginative delight, are part of a repertory theatre of the terrible and real. The gnome, the troll, bear the shadow of man, and are therefore not merely beings from folklore without a basis in human suffering.

The gnome   a twisted root
out of which "spirit forms" have been hacked—

trolls   the shadow work of ancient Europe,
the witch folds of early hybrid "Satans"—

the Buchenwaldans,
discovered by American soldiers, April 1945.

THE FIRST WORLD

Linked to indescribable power, to its shadow
analyzed by minorities who have, in my lifetime,
refused to remain anonymous—

"Until the missing story of ourselves is told,
 nothing besides told can suffice us;
 we shall go on quietly craving it."

Until now I read Laura Riding's statement as referring to
something I did not know how to disclose to myself about
my life. Tonight, "ourselves" rings communal.
What is missing: the rock against which
I might place my shoulder

    Allen Ginsberg's "queer shoulder to the wheel"

      Aimé Césaire's task may be Sisyphean,
but to be able to push for a people, that in and of
itself is significant resistance—

To write the disappearance of what I am?

Pushing my void as the comestible of ghosts to come.

ARIANA QUARTET

[7 October 2001]

Invasion of Afghanistan this morning.

passacaglia   grief and remembrance.

"Love one another or die" running through Beethoven's Quartet in
C Minor—a whole felt in any part, in any parting a hole melts.

John McGrosso's fingers on the finger board,
legs of an arachnoid, web-weaving frenzy,
each bow stroke a strand, cross-weaves by four,
opalescent orb
spanning the Ludwig branches.

Elf-entangled fleece of sound weaving back into itself, regaining its
animal, milk souring in its sweet, Shostakovich tarnish, yellow leaf
damp, an autumn otherwise without ash.

I know no one to mourn, so I mourn an infusion of an all
in whose broth always "It is Eshleman you mourn for."

The double-backed beast—"Death and the Maiden"—
giant leg pillow-bursting between the Towers
—varicose tanagers of bodies—

In my mind's lowered altitude
a scythe raves,
blackness marbelized with lips

"Lost bodies"
   not in conger-infested "middle passage"
but in hydra-mixed debris

music passes its rained-upon hand through.

[for Marcia Dalbey]

SONG

Cecilia Bartoli seems to taste her voice,
one moment a jowly barber, the next a gleeful coquette

As her neck muscles stretched
screwing her face up into a castle grotesque,
I saw a napalmed Vietnamese girl's face—

showing through voice as speeded-up waterfall,
voice as jewelfall,
                    the frozen O hole

    Scream strewn smile

In each scream
the screwdriver of early mind attempting to loosen
the bolt God sank into the rippling cuttable cords by which
song
spurts
dying

almost fuse.

THRENODY

As she smokes
the lit morgue of my heart mews
as she smokes
Apollo's shaft catches on fire
as she smokes
the verve of her gale is undercut
her hacking opens tunnels into her body's reserves
as she smokes
her place on the belvedere is taken over by a clown
as she smokes
a smoker necropolis greater than the populated earth sinks
    into view and yawns
as she smokes
all the burners are lit along Apollo's urethra
as she smokes
she vomits smoke
Terrifying is the light of Apollo!
It is never merely myth!
as she smokes
she waters her thirst with the best wine she can afford
as she smokes
her sphincter smuggles in more smoke
as she smokes
the sphinx in her chest turns into a gummy carburetor
as she smokes
I think of Kuwait's oil field opera of thick red scrolls,
    storied smoke, coiling crimson aircases, air as oil, a
    slick-blackened pelican stabbing at its breast
as she smokes
the Medusa shakes a rain of venom from her scalp
as she smokes
her lung cancer delights in being restoked
as she smokes

my love for her enters a desert on foot
her cavities turn into Camel-probed mines
as she smokes
Caryl is irked because I have joined her at the Duane Park
    Cafe bar, where she can smoke
as she smokes
I dream of shoveling live coals out of her back
as she smokes
in my desert I see a mirage of the Last Supper, a Stonehenge
    of 12 smoking camels, Nora as a wirey-haired Christ taking
    a drag from each disciple
as she smokes
as she grouches on the phone when I can't grasp her slur
as she smokes
as she takes a break to wipe herself under the reproduction of
    Guernica
as she lights up again
as she smokes.

ACROSS THE BERING STRAIT

Long bundles arching over stumps, tongues over
crumbling teeth, bundled poles over
hunched coals pouring, cinder by cinder forward...
I see Mary Ann Unger in death
still carrying glyptodontal loads,
the backwash of her life, her cancer,
her mastodontal desire to push on,
Siberian hunters at 20,000 B.P., moving several miles a year
across a 55 mile land bridge,
the linked and the loaded, following the great sloth,
the short-faced bear, following camels, yaks, tapirs,
ringed by the saber- and the scimitar-toothed, ice-browed
  humanity,
Unger sees them as bending tusks sprouting out of
mammoth-headed ice, the lurchfolk,
about whom we know nothing! For Beringia is gone!
Like a shrub-ox, or capybara, the land bridge,
with their footsteps, their middens,
the bones of the peccaries they killed—
homage to Mary Ann Unger, dead in 1998, a sculptor,
she grasped these lurching, lugging entanglings,
"Across the Bering Strait," the bearing of weight over time,
over the land bridge of a life,
wrappings, pilings, backpacks, loaded baby slings,
moving toward a mystical Organon, where all is organ,
a paradise of animals, following the crazyquilt meat drift,
to penetrate the animal realm, to get animal know-how,
humankind, like loosely tied poles, lurching on,
over boulder knolls, eating tundra smut,
gotta travel gotta follow the horns,
horn of a moose, horn of an elk, first flag!

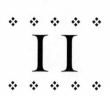

II

BLUE ZONE

I

Ann's ocean was above her head this afternoon.
We looked into it,   vast clear wispy blue skies,
turbulent plow under,   troughs and prairies. . .
Ann small under her ocean,
Ann with frail upper arms.

This ocean now takes on annihilational size.
We see tears move into the outside of Ken's eyes. . .
well that's what we see,   we see very little,
friends with chicken soup

(the poem hesitates to say more now,
to do so
would intrude on Ann's destiny)

II

Why didn't I grasp this earlier? Last week
after hearing of Ann's 7 hour emergency ward siege
I dreamed: my mother and father
full face in the dream screen,
me telling Gladys the bad news,
her curling away, accepting? Her shoulder
last seen, then Clayton
full face, a line of blood between his lips
as in the van Gogh Saint-Rémy self-portrait.
I saw Ken Mikolowski in my dream-father's face,
realizing I had brought my family forward
out of anguish for Ken and Ann.

III

Right before evening, the daily equinox.
Do the dead tap in now?

Thoughts of Ann, looking at bobbing
redbud shimmer flows,
drift of several branches, moored
Calder-like, frail green canopies.

Tidal fugue of the past building through the present—
to break, futurity foam.

Suddenly flashing across Ann's psyche.
I must be careful to respect its whitecaps, its pines.

IV

The savagery of reaping, of God
crushing crows in his hands to scatter across
poor Vincent at sea in the yellow-
rushing-toward-him-waves.

We are those sunflowers, Ann,
lifted into the grail oven,

immense black sunflower extending
as far as forever is.   Not "Here Lies"
                    but Here *standing*

    My sense of human
    goodness was raised
    in knowing you.

V

Standing by the sink before
half-shuttered kitchen window evening light,
striking a cleaver between lamb rack ribs
I thought of Ann,
arcane feelings moved in my body,
I was butchering what I had roasted and
Ann was failing,   I was gripped by
an airless symmetry,
I paused over the rack—
a kind of architectural design was present,
I thought back to our afternoon visit,
Ann's calm and humor, her daughter Molly's tear-repressed face,
Ken was north—
                    a design
organizing itself in space,
as old as a scratched line,   Ann's city of art
combining in the sky over Ypsilanti—
I saw cloud-like gates,
meticulous granular observational scapes,
each registered   as the structure itself.

VI

Ann in the dark of an all
I hardly reach metaphorically,
refused transport beyond metaphor's
   half-self.
           Ann in full passage.
I'm feeling the wall,
the fulcrum, the tilt beyond which
you will exist in memory

O radiant spider crawling with wounds

VII

Off Monhegan Island the basic blue
turned into courageous slate, shifting
diaphanes of melancholy aquagreen.
The azure has a metallic edge, a dun
    infected will.
                    In high ocean shadow
clarity's tiara became a nebulous mass,
a coma, a rain-soaked hyacinth.

The ocean's ground was chipped with locking tints,
inks and shields, crumbled steles
married to a verdigris
spotted and stained with forests
rising from a liquid core. . .

an undulant ground, blue gum streaked ruby,
russet and obscure, and then a modest larkspur
pattern appeared, a humorous blue,
as if Krishna's cyanotic body were the ocean's skin.
Through rolling bronze, a red archangel spread out in
    serpentine flails. . .

Unending transformation in a single frame.

Blues for Ann. Peacock meridians in repose.
Blue air over crocodile and cream.
Oyster whites flecked with jelly yellows.
A magnanimous blue, chilled by receding shades,
a tone at once a color and a mood,
peaks and troughs leveled into a glaze,
a frail synthesis shuddered by far-near thunder,
by gusts of ruddy, honeycombed winds.
A horizon crawling with serpent skirts of fire.

A repose at once milling and aligned.
The angel within the maze,
the maze within the angel—

courage   modesty   laughter   magnanimity
  an individuated blue

    your legend, Ann

VIII

Ann was sleeping when we entered,
aged
     by a week of operational agony.
Laid back facial planes,
nose too angular,
pursed, nicked lips,
          breathing,
her body small, under thin cover.

Caryl said: let's let her sleep.
So we went away, found a lounge, waited for 5 minutes.
I told Caryl Ken said it was ok to wake her,
so we went back.
          The pot of sunflowers
still in good shape after 5 days
against the window—beyond which: Ann Arbor in
  helpless, redundant green.

Ann woke and smiled through hell at us.
Caryl knew what to say. My glances pingponged about
Ann's bruise-mottled arms, moist swept-back hair,
the sweet nurse adjusting the yellow IV udder load.

We had brought her a beribboned little box of Queen
  Anne's cherries.
Ann quiver-nibbled, joking "as the queen,
I insist you taste my cherries."

We both touched her arm and left
the combined power of Ann's
smile and pleading gratitude.

IX

The recumbent is a vessel.
The attender a rotting god.

Ann's ocean floor profile enters my gut.
My brain attempts to revive her via
hallucinatory sleep—
everything an instantaneous metaphor,
sofa turning into cave organs,
sky a swamp, stars
the bursting lungs of catfish
—as if to transform Ann
into something else, the goad for
belief in reincarnation?

Ann
    underground.
Who
    visits now?

Love's absence-driven,
    love's presence-bereft,
humble before the art
    of earth's larder.

No release from this recumbency
    ceiling all face

the Sistine spread.

[June–September 1999]

BEDROOM, 6 AM

Bulbous rootwork of drape rings,
sleigh grey slides

    ceiling quilted ripples

City bus brakes releasing
—pigeon fluttermuffle—
lint of sounds. . .

We are young and beautiful to each other
posing for a snapshot,   Lespinasse, 1974,
we are flooding each other with the perfection of
   mutual reception,
there is a basement, a hallway, you are leading me
   past my parents,
there is Matthew. . . cows in Perigord fog. . .
dreams become visions. . .

Little canals of sunlight
saturate the curtain folds. . .

Your face from the bed extends,
your body goes out into the room,
to wake is to enter
the Caryl-enfabulated world.

ANIMALS OUT OF THE SNOW

When snow falls deeply,
mountainously, curvaceously,
animals begin to nudge forth. . .

Caryl and I were visiting the young poet Stephen Smith
in the world of 3 AM,
I was generating organs for a new book.
We were invited, as if for a cottage
or mountain cabin stay, but the beds were uneven,
things were tilting, for hours it seemed
I worried about my throat and
the corpse of John Logan
putting itself into my throat.

   At some point it was clear:
Stephen was out of control,
his pets would not behave, would not
let us sleep. Logan, according to Kessler,
was so incapacitated near the end of his life
that he lived in an armchair.
Bandit students wandered in and out of his ruined lord,
taking his penis here and there.
Caryl and I were increasingly nargled,
Stephen and Karen had vanished, the animals were
more and more active, angry, would
not let us sleep, slightly fantastic
then beaver-dog bizarre,
a cat covered with nipples, a pumice-faced
zippered pug,
                so I had to get us out,
we were now in a vast urban morgue
(earlier that day
our pantry began to drip,
snow on the roof produced yellow swellings off
   the upper moulding,
splot tears,   Caryl put out pans).

There are dream blasts that annul both
imagination and memory,
I was carrying Caryl naked blue and stiff,
carrying her like a forward-thrust figurehead torn from its bow,
then we were back at Stephen's, with the beasts—
they increased, no one could handle them,
blind hogs, serpentine chows,
tiny striped carnivores, snake-headed chihuahuas—
as Thomas might have said: it was early it was Adam,
I was scared out of my dream into
an exploding morgue of animal underdream,
we fled again,
                    finding ourselves by
a charred plantation by which
blacks were hunched on benches,
  "we can't help you" they said,
oh they were poorer than we, so
again we turned back, into

a stable aflame with molar loads,
with the lords of animal revenge?
I had no rudder, could not make myself awake
and start a new dream or
simply the Zukofsky codex
("we are going to sleep to sleep")
the quarrel, until I stabbed a hyena, was out of control,
out of ego's bathysphere,
again I awoke, begging to be awake,
Caryl had flung off her comforter,
spread-eagled in tee-shirt,   sleeping soundly.

"HOY LE HA ENTRADO UNA ASTILLA..."
—César Vallejo

Today the toothache-like pain explored
her left shoulder. Dusk light penetrates foliage
like this pain tendrils her body. That is,
the pain grows, a healthy fascist organization.
She has fought the pain with doctors, with vitamins,
with everything she can marshal. Earth
blunders through her, or sidesteps through her.
At times she can hardly move. In the same moment,
she is a spirited companion, regardless of her pain,
she offers the lattice of relationship—
love makes its way through the minefield of what
nature seems to have prepared. Who knows
the source of fibromyalgia? The Buddhists are wrong:
desire is not a blanket cause. Today
the toothache-like pain swept through her entire body.
I admired with my whole being the way desire was never
absent, in her eyes, her words, her bearing.

[17 June 1999]

IN HAPPINESS A POWER

There is in happiness a power that stems the maggot tide.
And not just dying, but the maggotry men invice in life.

When Caryl's face smiles forth, I think I briefly pass on,
or pass into the chill of passing crossed by permanence.

FOR DAVID WALDORF

Writing at
  end of day,   urine
falling,   edge of the stream
flecked, diamonded, horizontal
  dream chain,
helix evocation

"Do not go gently" inside the gold fall

David Waldorf accepts his terrible mental illness
because only through it
did he discover the holy depth of life—
Caryl and I watched him talk on the Creedmore Program,
having honed in on drawing while listening to
  late Beethoven,
the composer his spiritual companion,
deaf Ludwig,   composing in spite of deafness,
David,   often totally out of it,
  drawing, somewhat like Michaux,
smoky elfin calligraphic linking/disappearing
  figures,   psychically alive.
David draws when he "comes back"—
when he is "out" he doesn't know. . .

       an abandoned nest
on our porch,   two days of racket
  the energy of the brood peaked,
noisy flutter storms,

sagging sparrow nest,
you were no more than a launch pad.
How much human dysfunctionality = home too long?
How many live on in the dirty
abandoned parent nest?

No one knows where David goes when he is "out."
He returns, weeks later, "comes back."
I wonder if his body tries to find his mother body,
if he enters a centerless labyrinth,
when he comes to the labyrinth's void, if his body
translates this void into no-womb,
if the concurrent terror turns him toward
"coming back"...
     We are all blessed with
Ariadne's clew. The labyrinth's outer gate,
for most, is never bolted.
       Rich walls of this
world cave. Corridor bend of this redbud. Of
Caryl's neck. Of Waldorf's crayon. Stalactitic witch.

THE TUSK HOTEL

Lonely to death, totally engaged,
lifeless, snoring, I round the carnal cape and
bet on Africa, as the rift in my design,
the "western wind" by which I was driven from the trees.

Every poem could end here,
pointedly, on the ground,
yet every poem begins here,
baby sling packed with amethyst and memory.

Backdrop for the play called *My Unknowable Death*.
Backdrop billowing forth, elephantine peril.

We're registered in The Tusk Hotel.
Caryl and I share a double with an abysside view.
Every morning, in spite of what life is,
we ensnout our masks and ripple through the Flood.

A SPANGLED MOOR

To stop for a moment and think about writing at or into evening,
white wisp of plant tassel floats by the window—
the lid of dark infinite space has yet to be placed.

Sometimes evening opens and the beauty and complexity
  and complicatedness of Caryl's soul
makes all that I have wanted   sing—
in Les Eyzies I love to watch the light shut down,
or the dark grey through,   or my mother remain in conjunction
  with Caesar,
as I dream of poems that could change something essential
about the way a few people view creation...

Now 10 degrees darker than when I started
—predator twilight is oozing fertile annihilation through
Whitman's pores—there he is! still under Bunyan
who is giving Walt a wonderful blowjob and pulling at his
  beard and toes—
now what? The hour between dog and wolf,
where dog becomes foreign to what we dream to cover,
our bodies moving toward moving under,
ah, sheets, fresh sheets, a warm blanket, maybe
our beloved, or simply a friend...

I work a bit now, watching the spangled moor of my tundra
  dreams
soften and leaf-adjust to what I can offer.

A YONIC SHRINE

When I piss into your blood (paper decomposing, pink furls, red under-risings), I feel an aimless goodness, a fascination with decon-struction—then a new spurt, making a new pattern, sinks me back, joyfully, into the childhood sandbox.

There is something gorgeous about this blood and its odor, arcane, alien to my male snout, evoking Egyptian carnelian. I become the wall upon which I am often climbing. I watch myself, fascinated with a self that from this viewpoint is hopeless.

I'm a lizard guy whose eyes are in the soup as the cruelties of the brew climb into him. Then I am utterly intact and belong, not to anything in particular. It is a small, acute sensation.

Another slight shift. The lioness has gone up my nose. My hand around my basalt is involved with a Ka I am otherwise too American to divine.

So I flush—or if late at night, walk away back to bed—with a Munch Scream swirl, that molten to sallow nightshade, reconstruct-ing the possibility of a dream. Tonight I am at my desk, jotting this down. I'd prefer to be back in bed beside bleeding Caryl. She's asleep and it is good that she continues to sleep.

Feeling less than her rings, I breathe deeply and know I will be asleep before ten deep breaths, enfolded in nothing, with the sider-eal taint of that lexicon that is the basis upon which I can say:

In spite of everything, I love you, and I love the earth.

[27 February 1994]

SOME ROCK OFF WHICH TO TRAVEL

Light from the TV burnishing Caryl's shoulder.
11 PM, she's on her side, head pillowed,
I'm sitting up, stroking her back,   so the light
purls, or hesitates on her round
then greys into whatever,   I don't know. . .

I'm entranced by the tenderness I feel,
the almost-far-reach of TV light
furling, it seems, or pearling,
a ridge, a radiance, I'm so dumped in myself
thinking of the Dordogne,   some rock off which to travel. . .

What is this tenderness that glows right before sleep?
There is something disgusting about it
(a voice says) if not expressed during the day.
It is the eternal brink of lying down to sleep
(another voice) for you might not wake up,
she might not,   something in you says goodbye
every night before you crest—

into what? As if the day has been so active
it takes 11 PM to elicit humble love and worry,
sweetness and broken cordage. . .

INSIDE CARYL'S LEFT SHOULDER

Gleaming, half-housed in steel sheath, the debrider's rotary blade whirring, resecting scar tissue, flaked-away rotator cuff.

It is inserted via a trocar pushed through the portal cut into her shoulder.

Apparition of a whirly, round eye on the debrider as it swivels caught in the arthroscopic beam.

Octopus or shark eye.

The debrider now a kind of monster in a feeding frenzy.

Blobs of bloody tissue stream the video screen.

Feathery tissue flurries.

The mowing of Caryl's ocean floor.

From another cut that appears to have no trocar the cauterizer appears, spurting bubbly water as it prongs up tissue.

Amber tufts throbbing by threads.

Tentacle-sucker-like bubble chains.

Rose shadings, yellow, bronze, in the white densities.

What happens to her deadened pain?

She's out, but her body's experiencing what I see.

Faced by the ungraspable within my own making.

Again the debrider, a ferret into the baby rat nest of her shoulder, whirring forth what the cauterizer tore up.

Watching this silent 20 minute video as you rest upstairs.

Blood-tinged snow chamber.

Cave amber.

As if I am looking at calcite draperies.

Cosquer being ensouled.

Orchid-like tissue bunches, almost loose, the cauterizer hooking up cartilage.

Threads of blood from her humerus head spurting, snaking out, vanishing.

Humerus head framed by the octagonal lens.

Fleecy white skull.

The moon.

The debrider shaves what looks like skull hair—not head hair but feathery wisps clinging to a skull.

Beautiful grassy white skull.

The debrider mowing and mowing.

For a moment: craters   rilles   ghostly inverted nipples.

The burr with square steel cleats rasping her acromion, trimming its hooked edge that cut into a tendon and caused her such pain.

"Frozen shoulder," which for a month she could not move.

Others will watch arthroscopic surgery inside their beloved's body.

Others will wince and draw close to "heavy debridement and acromioplasty."

Others will be given access to the body's interior grottos, its blood strings jetting, its moon and cave scapes, the sudden black fissures that check the eye.

Others will project and know how I felt, respectful of projection while attempting to see through to the images forever emerging, as if trying to make contact with us, there where projection and something there and emerging meet, as an image is glimpsed in an undulant dimly-lit cave.

Yes, others before me, by juniper wick, watching creatures emerge, recede, Cosquer, 18,000 B.P., auks, seals, jellyfish, there and not there, spirits receding, emerging, in ochre outlines, blood-ribboned snow chamber.

Before a screen, outside your invasion, and the source of your invasion.

Alone and with you in this wild disturbance of your sense of physical unity.

Fox-like rotary saw in the hen house of your scar tissue.

Rapacious correction of the destruction of your enjoyment of life.

[for Mark Mijnsbergen]

54

SHOPPING

Crematorial sensation in a department store, thousands of suits and dresses without bodies, as if it is always Book 11 of *The Odyssey*, we are surrounded by speechless souls

Souls trying on souls, the hippo-assed white, the mantis-waisted black, caramel shoulders of a teenager, a pink ankle-length soul for Xmas day

Caryl found some fabulous pants, gold-green alligator quills, loose in the crotch, baggy in knee, she put them back, fearful no tailor she could find could alter them perfectly

(In eternity, Henry Miller is a tailor—
 lustfully he entered the Cave of the Nymphs,
 soon became concerned with the gates of ivory and of horn,
 souls arriving, souls departing, all needing a cutting here,
     a mending there—
 a drowned soul slithered in, needing resurrectional attention,
 old Blake hobbled through,   Henry dusted him off,
     perked up his lapel)

We sashay over to the Santa Center, the old sot in red crumples each wish, sending a beam of hope into the child heart, I can feel the soot already in the childrens' mouths as wishes like elves congregate on their lips, they sit for a moment on the stony gingerbread knee, this realm of sweet deception

Dorothea Tanning's female cloth-like forms blow through, crumpling knots of outwinding femininity

Department
  depart   meaning or
Beckmann's *Departure*
costumes awaiting casting off

Redesign yourself, step into this angelic armor

Cuddly music, emptiness made cozy

  "'Exquisite work, madame, exquisite pleats'
vanish into a bloated face, ordering more dresses,
   gouging the wages down,
dissolve into maria, ambrosa, catalina,
   stitching these dresses from dawn to night,
   in blood, in wasting flesh."

Old man in a pea jacket searching for something among womens'
suits

Recalls my father searching for my mother after she had died, he'd
steal his car keys the Rest Home people had hidden, then drive and
drive, 200 miles away one afternoon a housewife found him parked
in her driveway—when she asked him what he was doing there, he
told her he was looking for Gladys

Had he entered an Eleusinian frame, would Gladys have emerged
from the stranger's home in a purple, mushroom-encrusted gown?

—emptiness keeps coming in,
the unfillable sleeves and slacks of life

The terrible animal imprint in perfume departure, the civet cat,
the musk deer, crushed like grapes, displayed in tiny gold vases

I help Caryl shop, holding her coat and scarf, pick out clothes,
color schemes, purples, lavenders, auburns and deep browns, things
for her new silhoutte.

EVENING WITHOUT CARYL

The upstairs tonight without you—
the tarp-covered piled dirt by your mother's pit

in the Möbius-band of this audible silence,
as if each ear were a giant conch,   sea phones,
    sound of the interior of my blood—
        circulating head,
            her body in a recent dress
        as I undress,   I'm putting on
            atmosphere—

all *is* atmosphere,   one is never not touched by the hole,
        all, absence, fragment—
    my astonished body missing
pressure from the organic world
will cease to be contained,   as if the sack were pulled
        from a sack of sand.

Far away from myself,   from the noise of myself,
my heart yesterday was stopped by
Irene's heart,
    a yellow leaf brushed my palm,
her daughter's temporary absence   the feel of the leaf,
waxen, tender, unstemmed *thing* between fingers and thumb.

            The room as a vault,
wherein silence is jugular,   a growing invisible
    plenum,
                thuddings of shovel goodbyes.

Frail little woman whom I hardly knew,
but who raised my sweetheart,   whose body
    brought her to me—

O outside,
how *do* we remain congruent to you?

[10 October 1988]

SWEETHEART

Putting MSM cream on your back,
watching the white work into the gold,
shoulder blades, latissimus, the top of each shoulder,
wondering how this substance brings relief.

You stand naked on the bathroom mat,
grateful for an hour of minimal pain.

Feeling your flesh and bonework:
can fantasy and biography mesh?

It has been nineteen years since I wrote:
"You are oysters cigarettes a radio"
—third line of a forty line poem I couldn't finish,
each line for a year of your life.

Today I'd like to display your sweetness in strata,
bed upon bed, chrysalis and imago.

You are a bawling caterpillar, a puppy snarled in her own wings.

So tasty the incubus harpies have already spotted you from their
helicopter eyries.

In the 1946 VJ Night neighborhood celebration, a four-year-old
out alone, tasting beer, miraculously steered home.

At seven, you told nine-year-old Susan Brotsky and her mother
that you knew what a period was. Amazed, they said, "Well,
what is it?" "The dot at the end of a sentence."

By constellating and naming stars humans have tried to make them their own—but is there a mouse constellation? A constellation for your dog you named Chubby?

With hair set by your mother with water and sugar, what sweetness the bees tasted intoxicated by the little blonde lost in high grass a few yards from home.

Caryl Reiter with a dog-collar ankle bracelet. Caryl Reiter with slingback black shoes.

Caryl Reiter grown beyond pinafores in a stretchtop with a topless brassiere, nylons on Sunday because her Catholic friend wore them, in leopard pants, lipstick painted over her lips.

You stopped and talked with the poor soul masturbating under the Coney Island boardwalk.

With your cage of tamed bumblebees you inspected the human curfew as a messenger who would ascend the pyramid of Medusa without Athena's rearview mirror.

A staircase without a banister as a way of mastering the void.

Inside the LSD fortune cookie: "Kill the substances in order to find the retentions."

Months spent drifting Pluto with a wounded Scorpio who tried to sell you a constellation called "Tail o' the Torn Cat."

Raped, you refused your friends' offer to break the Greek's legs.

Met by wild pigs on a road without edges you sat down and caressed the force trampling you.

You dreamed you were a stone lady holding up a building. The only thing alive was your cunt, was there for lonely men, just to fuck them—if they knew enough to fuck you then they knew your cunt was alive.

I looked up, swam up into you, air.

We rented a Volkswagen one Sunday, spring 1970, drove to Harriman State Park and ate acid in the woods. Filled with that poison I began to shout for Hollie, my "new" Marie, another person I had chosen to desire as self-torture. We came back to the car at dusk, the parking lot filled with picnicking Puerto Ricans. You had your camera—we started taking pictures of each other over the back of the Volkswagen. Once, looking through the lens I saw you—Caryl—not La Muerte, femme fatale, or housewife, but an exasperated, sweating woman who was original! not the image of Woman, not superficial; fresh.

When you were married in your late teens to Alan, you told your mother you were taking ergot to abort. "It's not going to work," she said. "Why?" "Because I took it before I had you."

From time to time, as if from a dry basin of stillness, I hear you say: "I have nothing to do." Is that ergot moment the burn spot in your peacock ledger?

The chunks of jasper we collected in Utah—I keep three on my desk under the book shelf where the image of Faye Dunaway is assimilated into your specific loveliness.

Thoughts of you conjure the *granite rose* of Trégastel, undulant Daliesque near-forms tawny in mid-morning sunlight, or the dove-grey, ochre limestone cliffs wandered by long black stains as we approach Les Eyzies on D47 from Périgueux.

Lespinasse, 1974: we carried our dinner outside to the stone table on the landing by the door to our second floor Bouyssou apartment. The farm was on a rise which sloped down through an apple orchard. When we sat down to eat, well before sunset, we had for entertainment an extraordinary sky. Clouds would come floating over the woods, spreading out over us. Puff collisions, Mickey Mouse ears, shredding gargoyles, turrets, vales, mammoth apparitions densifying and disintegrating as they appeared. Many reminded us of the images we were trying to make out on the cave walls. To sit at that stone table—what an experience— to be in love there, at one of the most vital times in our many years together. Much of what happened—the "event aspects"— during our first spring and summer in the Dordogne is now as dispersed as the clouds we used to watch—yet it billows in us, an inclusive cloud whose heart is ours.

Getting up in the middle of the night at the farm you spotted a large lavender spider in the middle of the kitchen floor. You let out your spider scream, and the spider, making tapping noises on the linoleum, ran under the stove. The next morning, after trapping the spider in a shoe box and removing it from our apartment, I ate a small live spider to calm you.

Out of the compost the silver the blue and the silver the gypsy holocaust and the fifteen aromas of any word and listening and listening to the scrapes of the scarab trying to motion that the wedding is *down there*.

"How do you feel about your body?" the LA physical therapist, after asking you to take off all but your panties, inquired. Your answer as you stood before him was, for me, Aphrodite ascending.

You presented me with one solution to the Jack and Jill conundrum: he cracks at orgasm because he goes to fulfillment with an empty pail.

62

Going over worksheet after worksheet with me, at the table in the
morning after coffee, asking me thousands of questions: what did
I mean by this, why did I write that, helping me to narrow down
the infernal discrepancy between what I thought I had written
and what I did write. While I went into the labyrinths on my own
and sometimes emerged, at the center you were the companion
providing resistance, neither Minotaur nor Falconress.

At night, from your North American belvedere, you see your
returning bees, loaded with wingless Guatemalan bees, waver
and drop into the unregenerate heart of man.

Devonshire, 1979: your utter accessibility, your head tilted under
green apples, your sweetness sweetness, your tart light heart-
sown, your hair blown sweetness.

I love to watch you eat fresh Dungeness crab—your plate heaped
with cracked ice, topped by a reconstruction of the crab. Over
which your delicate fingers—more delicate than the morsels
you will extract—pause like wands, and you slowly eat, as if you
were undoing a sewing, as if your fingers are needles investigat-
ing music, or thinking about "The most sublime act is to set
another before you," which can refer to any act of respect for
the otherness all nearness is, not to be worshiped but revered in
motion, in pleasure scythed and harvested, a beautiful creature
eating a beautiful creature.

You've made a half-dozen photo collages with us, friends, and
places. In the downstairs bathroom today I stopped before you
in your Italian blue jump suit with flared legs and sleeves (in
which you danced upstairs at Max's Kansas City). On another
wall there's a photo of you smiling in the raccoon coat I bought
for you on St. Mark's Place—you're wearing it with my crushed-
velvet rust pants, wide leather belt, and scarlet sweater. The fur
turns henna in the 1969 autumn sunlight.

I look for words for what being inside you is, the thought makes
me shake, empty quivers like Songs of Songs volley about. To
place myself inside you and not hurt you, to be at the heart of
your life, to slightly know you where only you know yourself, to
have this billygoat extension encased, a warm oar as if in the
first the very first waters.

After dinner, 1982, in a Paris bistro otherwise forgotten, a dog
jumped up next to you on the banquette, sat there, looking up
politely, a pug, big ET eyes, smashed truffle nose. Just sat there,
happy. So I went out to the kitchen and asked about the dog.
The chef said: "he stays with me in the kitchen until I finish cook-
ing, then goes out into the restaurant and chooses someone to
sit by. He's Belgian, a Brabançon. The males are good-natured
the females are very bitchy. They have small bottoms and have
to deliver a big head."

Your assemblage in the dining room corner: on an old ironing board a
wooden skateboard holding up your sculpture of my head in un-
fired clay, flanked by a stuffed rabbit lady and a photo of a white
gorilla. Beyond, at each end of the skateboard, a *tanuki* with
ground-length balls, sake jug, and chin-tied straw hat—and a pot-
bellied Balinese wood frog with a leaf parasol. Scattered about on
the ironing board: a clay Oaxacan lady holding a duck and a
squash with a cut watermelon on her head by Joséfina Aquilar,
many little pigs (falling on their backs, doing head stands), a 19th
century iron that used coal, a rabbit with a carrot candlestick, and
a salt and pepper set of two little fat rabbits. It is my *ofrenda*.

Your gold ring which you designed and cast, with its undulant
creased leaf base mounted with a rosette encased with a garnet
and a half-moon of seven tiny diamonds; across the diamond-
less third of the rosette, a furrowed sweep of gold, carotene
river as close to me as the Styx.

[1981–2001]

IV

BRANCHWISE INTO ZETA

Looking up our west red maple: rose-stained
   yellowing leaves. Beyond:
our lives in tapering branchlets,
   a myriad of cave ends.
                When we enter a cave
 sure of its termination—
                  we draw in our own rootstock,
bring the root baggage with us. We are
   psychically encoiled with our rootage,
our root meritage, our pebbles and
                our burials.
                    Autumn skims
the growth rust from our schemes, makes for wonder:
maiden wraith pile-driven scale queen
       Word jams,
        subconscious lore
I don't hear in spring.

are you the tepid pustulant of a crown yet to be crushed?
are you the mitre-scam, the infant ant skittering along
   these veins?
                Why this excitement
peering branchwise into zeta?   O
   this maple is a grail!

ARISTOTLE'S LANTERN

Someone has carefully, lovingly, with great illustrational spirit, made these drawings in *Webster's Second International Dictionary*. I have been unable to find a credit for these pictorial illustrations I have looked at, sometimes daily, for many years—my father's dictionary, kept in his slaughterhouse office until he retired.

The aardvark is crouching; the aardwolf is poised, on delicate toes.

The Acadian owl is bewildered.

You would not want to meet one of the Acarina (which cause horse mange): a tiny multi-tendriled root, a mask, with no eyes or mouth, tubes everywhichway.

The addax waits.

So does the adjutant—on one leg.

The agouti, out for a stroll, lifts and curls back a left front leg.

The wandering albatross, named after a Greek jar, appears to be firmly planted on earth.

One of the Amphipoda is thinking: Christ, how did I end up here?

The angwantibo, a small lemur with a rudimentary tail, crouches on a branch, right paw raised.

The ant bear appears to be two animals in profile grazing.

Bunch anticlines together and you get an anticlinorium. Or a caterpillar. Or peristaltic brickwork.

Jackal-headed Anubis holds forth a lance vertically, tip down. From his other hand, held behind him, an ankh hangs. His loincloth is the beginning of fashion. He has a dense black tail.

The aphis wolf (a kind of aphis lion who feeds on aphids) carries about a shelter made of aphid skins. Olson with his house on his head.

I left out the aoudad, a wild North African sheep, with a beard the full length of his or her chest.

A nearly male Aphrodite clutches her sheet-like clothing, wadded and falling down around her butt.

The Apneumones cannot breathe.

The apple tree borer, portrayed affronte, is displayed over a horizontal diagrammatic drawing of her larva.

The apteryx is nearly bald, most of his hair pulled out, leaning forward, bill down, a sorrowful Edward Dahlberg.

The arabesque (child of acanthus and palmette) is only an expressionless profile, left hand thrust forward, right toe thrust back. The rigid, vertical left leg looks like the beginning of architecture.

Have you ever seen an archaic smile?

Aristotle's lantern = the five converging jaws and accessory ossicles of a sea urchin.

PRE-CAMBRIAN ROSE

Joanne Verlinden has sent us
in her place
a small, single rose,
pitchblack but for the shifting
scarlet glow of molten
rocks,
      the cooling earth
here a dark red
palimpsest to my palm,
a spiral petal flow

out of Kali-Ma's
ocean of blood,
out of Set's soot
liederwoven.

[18 August 1999]

CRANIOLOGUE

Wearing my reconstructed mask
I rest, a 90,000 year old skull.
Having been tumbled by Olson, Pound, Williams, and Homer,
my age is ridiculous. You can't begin to grasp me,
even my youth. In the Border Cave I have to tell you
hyenas and porcupines worked over my skeleton.
Only my cranium remains, thus the epic and the long poem,
thus the attempt to write into paradise.
On the frontier between South Africa and Swaziland
I ponder tectonic shift,
and darling I must tell you I also wonder about
the Panama Isthmus which Steven Stanley claims led to
my presence, I mean its lifting to seal
the Atlantic from the Pacific some 2.5 million years ago,
eliminating woods where I clambered and climbed
as Australopithecus, meaning I had to evolve or die,
and most of me died, my life was and is
at the hands, nay at the uterus of the planet.
I had to come down, be terrestrial and deal with
sabertooth, a horror unknown until the 20th century.
The gist is I converted, invented a baby sling,
made use of my foetal-surge brain,
learned to bond, and to shape rock.
I am much more successful than you who read me,
I speak, as a kind of gay son of rock,
or the pore of one origin,
frozen, immensely disadvantaged, but an acute
failure the poets have had to transform.
All long poems lead back to me,
not heroics, or the tragic eclipse of love,
dryness, darling, meant I went on,
I and my columbines, my radiant nicked progeny,
thus I also speak as the gay daughter of rock,
for as a 90,000 year old, no one can locate my voice box,
my crinkum-crankum, or dingus. I disappeared into you, or

into the prototype of you,
my mask is calcium white and I did not ask for it,
I would have preferred to confront you as
Atlementheneira, one of my names in the now-called
Dordogne, only 30,000 years ago.
But neither the visionary nor the personal
can account for the planetary omega of my skull
nor the 20th century white mask
lending it the dagger-chin of so-called humanity.
What gets me about the Panama Isthmus ascending
and via conveyor belt winds
creating the Ice Ages is
that the oldest myths I know of
involve a cosmic dive of animals or shamans
bringing up earth from the depth of primal seas.
Is there a dream that old?
Can it be found? Or must I muse here in a drawer
that the oldest dream or vision has
under it that rising Isthmus?
Absolutely fantastic! Unbelievable!
As am I, perched, as a photo, in a book,
a *Homo* link, a homunculink,
my skull a rise, no more,
something lifting into view,
land bridge, the creation of human kind
masked by white that is surely the void.

SPARKS WE TRAIL

Profiled on whitish-ochre calcite:
5 antlered stag heads,
necks vanishing into an imaginary river,
file toward Lascaux's depths

Bodies unsketched on brown rock
as if river obscured

The first, head tilted, appears to be stepping up onto a bank

The second, head held high, must be walking the river bottom

The third and the fourth, noses lifted, must be swimming

The fifth seems to be faltering, sinking into

Mu-ch'i's "Persimmons" come to mind:
the emptiness in fullness as the stain of the real

We fill in the bodies of the stags, the water they are in,
so empty are our heads

Their heads of stone
lighter than we
weighted with mortal blight

This coming into appearance, this blooming, this full moon and
the tired sparks we trail as we disappear, stages of the crossing to
be filled in, suddenly total, emptying manifesting emptying, rever-
berating fore and aft vibrations

Suddenly noon—more suddenly, twilight

Or that other light Jacques Marsal spread across the antlered heads—I strained to see what was below: dark, cloudy rock, waterless rock, waterless water. Their below: unsketched

They are in the below
but   there's a deeper below

The limestongue off which stagstalk is struck.

THE HYBRID IS THE ENGINE
OF ANIMA DISPLAY

The earliest image of the soul appears to be
seated, or resting, within a bison-headed man.
She has an adolescent body, her face is slanted hair lines,
long head hair streams out his hump.
Her thin forearms slope forward and merge with
his human penis. They share three legs,
two knees lifted, as if dancing behind
the inflated anus of a reindeer which
swerves its aurochs head to gaze at this anima in her crib,
sharing the bison-man's spine,
suggesting Kundalini and that
animal forms were in sync with androgynous churning
while such figures acquired animal familiars.
Out of her forehead a leg-like limb twists, descends.
Comets zoom through it. Bison-man's tail,
same line-weave as her long hair, flaps their legs.
Out of his snout two lines of force extend and bow:
breath? blood? a sound bow
crossing his two held-forth animal-leg arms?
The three-in-one are readable unreadable,
they are, along with the reindeer-aurochs on whose rump
a ghost is perched, of
an unfolding matrix, envisioned at
a moment of initial pleats.
I thought: the sorcerer is a tub in which dead mom is bathing.
Yes, but such a perception is based on recent folds.
At Les Trois Frères, around 14,000 years ago,
the hybrid is the engine of anima display.

HYBRIDITY

Whose lion face is mangled with stripes of bison fortitude,
whose smoke body coils, ascending in descent, back curved,
neither man nor animal. . .

I am studying the figure carved into a stalagmite,
the Castillo cave, around 13,000 B.P.,
its verticality suggests man,
the way it emerges is what draws me,
this roily commingling of natures,
what comes up in me at night,
marvelous hybridity as the wedding in the dark,
Hades covering Persephone while Lawrence's scrawny
    ghost looks on,
as I sleep coiled by your thigh
as you sleep coiled by mine.

Now snowploughing into centripetal Yang,
"Lachrymae Christi" the archetype.
The catch of nascent form in Castillo my neighbor,
this movement in the night I'll call bilharzia,
like kudzu spreading throughout the body politic,
and then a creational alm like a self-proliferating salmon,
the moon strikes and our bodies go gaga with futurity,
I begin to rove in your thigh
—are you roving in mine?

The poem is an amoebic constellation involving
    all scattered lore,
it is where we coincide and evaporate,
vanishing into presences we discuss at morning.
The carving at Castillo is a dream erupting on
    a battered erection,

it is a sac relaxing out of a vagina,
it is moonlight and protocol,
bison jam, curling like smoke over bones ripe
   with fissures and pores,
gore that in dream seeks to be less crucifixion
than these half-way prisons between material and form,
I is so loose it can attach to a leaf like scale,
image is a dream sac of moonlight, it smells of jam
as it roasts in mind's vegetal oils,
it is curd, it is Odin nailed
and flavored, a welt developing on a branch,
a wounded skunk, charcoal lichen, a tongue in lizard trance,
all true images are incomprehensible,
   (false ones are fat wallets),
true images are I mage collapsings,
animal robes out of which scalpels are proturding.
The subconscious will only ascend so far,
it will lift like a crocodile's back,
belly always under, jellyfish belly,
tentacles out into the Suez Isthmus mud,
I see 50 start across, out of Africa, it is 100,000 B.P.,
50 *Homo sapiens*, they move like a loosening
centipede of fern-like foraging,
the earth is putting forth an image,
the stem of us, an image boiling up on a stalagmite,
trickle of a band, what did they dream?
Did luminous stalagmites rise in their sleep?
Did ruminate stalactites descend?
Ah, the early imaginal chewing, breaking
down worlds, extracting their fusional juices!

GRANDE CASCADE

  Out of the mother
urn the now ending
evers churn, they rhyme only
because I am free
here in fatal Gladys light. Let my kneeling
radiate my aging elfin sails.
Inbunched, outerflowered,
I am the hiss in this, the ripple wild
knoll in which my umbilicus sucks stones.
Paradise is part of my inherited billabong,
its stagnation, its warpings, are not my own.
Dionysus, let me not reduce or simplify,
allow me the wavering
miraginality of imagination,
let my fits and bits and catatripe
be venomous to the fake.
The body is a ruthless tribal compression.
Dreaming is less free than imagining,
for the dream factory has a quota:
certain roles are paid less,
someone has always forgotten to
oil the compost crank, the elf who runs
the umbilical bandsaw is always AWOL.
Every perception
enters an imaginal file, buds in arrest
until swayed by a life-shifting rain
or the blight of the news of
an unknown person's death.
For psyche, all bets are on nothing.
A fist slammed against the door
reappears as an eel in mourning.
A turtle who has just taken the veil becomes
the wind-filled sail of a wooden tub
in whose sudsy water one discovers one's genitals,
eggs to be fried on Caravaggio's canvas.

The vague is as crucial as the definitive,
the wave a part of the pier.
Whose genie does not accordion into Fudd and Marilyn,
then rebottle into Lautrec's cognac-
vialed cane? Clouds are brains,
chryselephantine scrolls,
or so the mind registers its Matterhorns
half-waking out of dream, when snow and sneezing
are as relevant as the cut rose
you place in my hand every time you speak.

RIFF

Torrid July with its mottled shadow dazzlings,
the center is out there—
the circumference: this daily mail of silk-sack clouds,
clouds like meal drift, moulded over, melted,
sheep flock clouds, worlds of wool,
torn tufts, tossed pillows,
clouds that flaunt forth, chevy on an air-built
   thoroughfare,
                 "Parisian Thoroughfare"
paideuma of Hopkins and Powell,
under bop paws the modal floor
"Wreck of the Deutschland"   "Un Poco Loco"
sprung projective verse, sprung bop,
dear tinny piano against
the stadium of the inscape,
   chain mail play gale

—upon what do poets improvise?

A via negativa octopodal in its outreach,
speech fiber sled
dragged by Hades' huskies toward auroral rage,
the rage to in rising not lose infernal coals,
improvisational aurora,
to live in a rarified gondola,
to be fully touched,
to feel the summer extend through   yes, Kosovo,
rape-body poisoned wells
rewiring Hopkins' windpuff bonnets.

MY DEVOTION

I asked, and was taken in a roundabout way to angels.
One held forth an orange-gold fruit,
        the fuzz was feathered,
chickadee orange. Eat, the angel commanded.

I bit into liquid silver
heavy and cool, streaked with amber light—
blood butterflies
flitted
vertically rippling
ferned eels. . .
Was this the "cosmic soul" of the alchemists?
The "white skin" of the "upper water"?

Earlier that night, I touched Caryl's cheek in the car,
the softness was metaphysical.
What did I touch? Her dearest sensing?

Before an answer might be given, swept on by
animal-shaped clouds, I was deposited in a grove
where a unicorn was grazing.

Across void-punctuated perceiving,
to reach a composite gift.
My finger   a unicorn
        grazing paradise

MORPHOLOGIES OF PARADISE

"I soil the paper to prepare it
for hallucinations. I reverse the
day's attempt to assassinate me."
—Matta

Shamanic jimson in everyone, the human Xibalba
a cosmogonic patch where twisting language retwists,
metaphorizing at the speed of dream, touching
the opaque shoulders of smoking trees, lighting
campfires in the backs of gigantic caterpillars.
This perception of paradise, first apprehended in
the Upper Paleolithic, I experience asleep,
via dreaming. Paradise is close, so close as to be
maddening. Paradise is in our brains.

What Blake calls Albion is this ancient creative zone.
The Fall is not original sin,
the Fall is that abyss between here and original imagination,
which we inherit as shamanic longing.

As one attempts to cross an abyss, metaphors
transmogrify so quickly
the initiate's receiver jams, loses its bearing,
deconstructs, like those divers
making their way through the 500 foot
waterfilled tunnel leading to the Cosquer cave—
the silty kicked-up sediment blinded them,
they lost their way among submerged stalagmites,
     drowned.

In the 1940s, the 20th century broke in two.
A revised version of hybrid man
—Auschwitz and Lascaux in the same brain—
complexed its obsession with "homeland."
Fueled with primal glory and Zyklon B, it sings:

"I'm always trying to get back
to my little caul shack on Ancestor Delta.
If somebody else—Kosovar, Arab, or Jew—
    happens to be there,
I'll claim *he is air*, and plant my fangs
    in his 'absence.' "

I sat down on the steps of The Ivory Tower and wept. The American's Guatemalan husband had not only been kidnapped but tortured and murdered. She doesn't know but knows, her 11 year old son is nearly cross-eyed with knowing, and I know, sitting on the bed edge, before PBS 12. Trying to gag her terror and grief, so as to be able to carry on with the interview, she finally pulls her blouse up over her face—as if to teach me another dimension of "the faceless woman" said to crouch on a bridge below the roots of the World Tree. I dream of lifting up this head, and assessing its weight, knowing full well it is impossible to weigh the unending assault on womens' bodies and personalities by the guardian husbands and brothers.

"Be forever dead in Eurydice."
Be forever reborn in Persephone.
A run runs through the morphologies of paradise.
Boogie-woogie of our diagrammatic sentence:
death and the possibility of redemption in
a single act.

For 1500 years, Eleusis, spiritual homeland of the Greeks. What *did* the initiates behold—which they were sworn on the penalty of death to not reveal—in the Telesterion?

    1] An ear of corn reaped in silence?
    2] A cereal wafer, the seed-*kore*, which they ate?
    3] The Divine Child, or Savior, variously named Brimus, Dionysus, Triptolemos, Iasion, or Elenthereros the Liberator,

83

laid in a manger (or winnowing basket), whose flesh was
eaten by the initiates in the form of bread, made from the first
or last sheaves?

4] An artificial vagina, kept in the *cysta mystica*, which they
touched?

5] An omphalos, or birth cone, representing the cervix, with fruits
and flowers, and a child emerging from a horn of plenty?

6] The spirit of Persephone herself, returned from the dead with
her new-born son, conceived in the land of death?

Whatever they beheld—since it was said to bestow happiness, the
true life, freedom, respite from all troubles—must have confirmed
to them: *after they entered the earth they would rise again.*

And who knows as well what the sacred king saw
the instant the goddess veil was lifted—
an afterlife? The origin of life? A scowl-vale of eternal grey?
Ah, dear tricky veil, you make us think, quest,
you are the rent/unrent conundrum
provoking our initiational probes to translate
the plutocracy of the literal.
Not to lift or rend, but to translate the veil.
The head of Hercules must be veiled
for the god, via omenta symbolics, to be reborn.
Yet we know that rebirth too
    is a halfway house.
                    No one has been to death
and returned to say: Emily is there, following her fly,
or, Artaud is happy, he has learned to bowl,
or, Pinochet is a 60 jab-a-second forked barbecue.
Dear veil,   speak to us of your fiber origin!

"We, the Mothers of Lascaux, extracted
fibers from celestial plants, located
the entheogens, set undulating
broken lines as coiling winds, winding torrents.
Channels of moisture circulated in our mouths
imbuing thread-like fibers with helicoid strength.
By opening/closing our jaws, working
our entire faces, while breathing, we formed sound
    strands,   speech lattices,
what you call the revealed Word, the veil word—
thus to lift the veil is an act we Mothers disavow.
To lift the veil would be to see the earth
naked, speechless, as on the first day,
amidst the chaos of origin, fiberless spirit,
    the not we knotted."

CEMETERIES OF PARADISE

Said to Caryl at day's end: this is home,
and then an aurochs wavered, or
was it shadow across the bulging
Les Eyzies cliffs? Bulging stone,
bulging horns, curling home. Lotal twisting
chambers where zero flexes.

The gate is open. Miller perceived some of the fix:
paradise is not of the French, is truly
Upper Paleolithic, of the Dordogne,
of the poets, to be reclaimed by the poets.

This is perfect, I felt,
making love in our farm apartment, spring 1974.
A bit north of Les Eyzies, the enchantment begins:
shadowing the curling single lane road,
moist outcroppings of limestone walls.
Out of the rock endlessly fabling.
Root wisps, black stains. My aurochs ancestor hovers.
We share a phallus, as if part of a carousel.
Slowing for a curve, up and down,
my aurochs ancestor on our turning shaft,
bird and fruit bodies on a common bend.
Uroboric carousel. Drifting into origin, or
into origin's coals, into the lifting off heat,
the dusty run-over, the psychic gore
alive in such caves as Combarelles.
It was in connecting with the mystery of a land
underscored by the most important thing I could learn
—the origin of poetry—
that bowled me under.

They entered earth to rise again.
Inside stone, no animals, blackness without stars.
By juniper flame, honey-colored ramparts
to be incised, brooded, crawled away from
back to tundra and frosty light.
Did this "round trip" resonate *resurrection*?
Did stone animals imply mortality could be broached?
Was scratching an enclosing line *resurrection*?
A proto-shamanic dream of healing form?
"I conceive and depict the bison I am to be"
Or was the marking of a bison as slain *resurgence*,
   a form of "resurrection"
uncomplicated by our "rising from the dead"?
I am suspended over such questions
   as over an abyss.

Line animating stone. Incipient alphabet.
At what point did the sound lark
split open to reveal a letter,
inkfaceting our dreams?

I crack open to find my
life. As if the word

stone were nut,
I must invent the kernel,

there must be life in my shell.
My rite must yield. Unlike Olson,

I do not "hunt among stones."
I hunt inside stone.

I work the manganese that holds, withholds.
In the end I hunt for more end,

of the beginning
I scrutinize each ochre start.

To be in paradise and to feel paradise at
an impossible remove. To crawl
the cemeteries of paradise. Rock
once alive, god bone.
Flint burin then as a tattoo needle to
    a human back today.

I sit on a green metal bench on
now-called *Rue de la préhistoire*, facing
Hotel Cro-Magnon.

To get at the round,
the jagged round of any situation,
how we fence with the udders of snow!

A complex of rainy perfection clears itself through me.

Packed with perpetuity's
negation, with swaying wordflora,
the alpha veil still refuses to unravel.

for Guy and Gizella Etienne
for celebratory hours at *Maen ar ya*

ERRATICS

                    Reality is a feminine wall
soft and cloud-like, a white Hermitage with a skeleton
    of steel.

❖

Now no poem wants to end.

Closure is
a precipice into Texaco
Du Pont   US Steel   the robot particles
    of a limbogator
acrawl about the planet.

❖

Winding through my language,
the delicate tentacle of an infant's mouth seeking
a maiden camel
on which to cross.

❖

To be inside Robinson Jeffers' Hawk Tower is to be inside his
knobby, tight mind. Steep narrow steps, embowering a music
room for Una—a Beulah haven within the cragginess of Robinson's
distancing angel. Tower that is menhir, tombstone, cross. Gigantic
honeycomb torched by Yeats. Rocks dragged from the Carmel
shore. The weight-lifter finding in the air a berth for his life load.

❖

Poetry, a nativity
poised
on an excrement-flecked blade.

❖

Orgasm
   drops me
for a second
               out, and it is my business to know
the no nature of this out,
which I suspect today
is the concretization of sunyata,
the body   gong of the void
the soul   in reverberation
clambers back to its bones,
its Cro-Magnon bones,
for also, in orgasm, all bones are
   on loan.

❖

Overlooked, the barren ground under November evergreens
   outside of St.-Bonnet-le-froid.
Overlooked, over-ripe fly-agarics and cèpes tucked under
   spruce boughs beside the path to La Fayet.
Overlooked, the scab-colored, stone-crawling earthworm
   in the chilly dusk.

Overlooked, my leather-and-wool-layered body.
Overlooked, the thickness of time,
                    the instability of being.

                         ❖

A photo seen in Peru, 1965: a hole in the ground around which
severed linking arms, four in all, were two on each side. The colo-
nized indigenous. Severed embracing arms around a pit of death.

                         ❖

   Infants who, unlike Australopithecus,
could no longer
cling to the mother's body hair.
A baby sling
out of animal tendon, at the beginning of the Pleistocene.
Perhaps the earliest sling.
Cobble or skull cradle,
slingshot,
subsequent spear-thrower,
tension point on the bow thong against which the notched
arrow catches—

   did a baby sling
carry first mind
away from the jaws of *Dinofelis barlowii*?

                         ❖

Looking at Hans Bellmer drawings:

Nippled doorknob

A woman vomiting a thermometer

The pelvic gaze

Oneiric orgy on a scaffolding enfolding Baudelairian lampreys

Possession as permutational symmetry

Lingual oysters roving in a sole

Under a cafe table sprouting bat wings: Hydra's smile-sewn skull

Masturbating the fifth and lowest breast

Inside the scrotal pile-up: The Holy Crater

Pulling open her belly brickwork to inspect the foetal lounge

❖

Wallace Stevens, why did you describe revolutionaries as "hairy-backed... hump-armed... serpent kin... in clownish boots... a little sly"? Such is right out of the Latin American versions of Disney comic books. Why did you write to Latimer in 1935: "The Italians have as much right to take Ethiopia from the coons as the coons had to take it from the boa-constrictors"? Or say to Cole, at the 1952 National Book Awards: "This is the poem that mentions the womb. I can't even pronounce the filthy thing." Is the exotica you loved to mouth, your "coo coo coo rou coo coo," the sound of tribal peoples disappearing as I write?

❖

A bison of redbud leaves stuttering in torrid 5 PM sun. Ghost bison. Soon to be ghost tree? Holocene extinction now inadvertently picked up in poetry: concreteness blown through by theory pellets; self-proclaimed sensitivity gaps. Buffalo Bill on a train platform taking out metaphor buffalo by buffalo.

❖

Gods buried in their burdens labor each day to die into
the design.

❖

I crawled into the field of my mother's vibrations. I was summoned by the beacons of her closed eyes. The vibrations became the labyrinth of my unconscious, a white ant hill, the queen of which is unknowable.

❖

I write below
a wasp nest
strung to the ceiling,
immense weightless grenade of masticated fiber,
inner walls honeycombed with tiny samurai
frozen this past October—

my work here is to bury
and keep alive
a fertile queen.

❖

In the flesh mauve of dawn
to read my palm as air, as atomic
impress, a lightmare,
as if I were shamanistically
constructed,
a vine of crystalline lore,
the tendonwork of cathedrals
sighted in life line talus.

❖

Nothing incapable of image. For a moment, no moment abstract. I
am of paradise. I have seen my dream, have seen through its dream
of remaining a dream. Argillaceous veins show through this body
stripped of Indiana armor. A Cro-Magnon shield reflects the shad-
ow convulsions of the primal image scene.

❖

The death of God sure takes a long time to fail.

❖

No one has returned from death
—other than Saint Generalization.

❖

Hart Crane drank to split open the ayahuasca cantaloup he thought was packed with god tongue. Or if not tongue, reptilian dictators resting on the lower depths of his brain. Were a split to have occurred, to whom would the dictation belong? To the anacondas or to Crane? Poets warm their livers at the crossroads of a dilemma that draws and quarters imagination. Poets camping there, squatting, as if in disembowelment, reading their interiors for signs—of the Divine?

❖

Faceless Laussel raises her blood-filled vaginal horn.

Drink from your own eyes.

❖

"We've gotten the halo out. The head is still inside."

❖

BELOVED (the film)
is an African-American Noh play.
A stranger arrives, slanted
as if buried standing up,
crawling with beetles,
a living nadir—

brought in, this jaw of mayhem
bubbles gruel, speaks in male bass,
a spirit returned to realize its fate,
to dance its agony that,
before it appeared in the flesh, was poltergeist.
The rub of BELOVED is: the ghost gets pregnant,
taking to the beyond (where it must return)
a baby to be born in soul,
or hell, Ariadne's babe,
eyes that look through a dog's eyes,
the look in a white man's eyes
that says, on a cosmological recorder,
I   cannot be reached.

❖

EMILY: What the fuck are you doing in my hopscotch?
ANTONIN: I'm fighting the zodiacal hyenas that created
     these traps!
EMILY: Have you a problem with my British sky?
ANTONIN: Have you a problem with my organless body?
EMILY: Rimbaud is making mincemeat of us in Abyssinia.
ANTONIN: Rimbaud stopped writing poetry because he got
     close enough to paradise to learn that he could not
     get in.

❖

As I stooped to slide the salmon in to bake,
a cardinal
vermilion shot
the redbud
its wreath.

❖

Artaud in a phone booth,
between Marquis de Sade and Savonarola,
trying to dial belladonna

as they burrow into him,
de Sade to draw out his sphincter,
Savonarola to wringer his heart

   sadona   de dada   arola
savosartona   rotolaaaa

the booth filling with Araudanola
   blood.

❖

Chinese mountains downed in moss
geese insectile

From dynasty to dynasty
day dark mist pervading grass-
cloaked fisherwomen pulling up a raft-
sized catch

Creative life as punctuation to nature's
calligraphic brambles.

❖

Train whistle sirenic through Ypsilanti, industrial, rusty, as if brakes
were being applied to the engine's genitals. Pipe organ constricted
while in full expansion. Tabernacle slaughterhouse factory sounds
in a single screaming clangor.

❖

Cool grey September flow through the chestnuts, leaf flutter so
intense no single leaf can be outlined. Dazzling like the sparking
milling of cuneiform fragments the backs of my hands release
pressed into my closed eyelids—all of which resolves into a dough-
nut of light, with a cenote-black center, the outer ring of which
seems bounded by astral dark. Is this the deep cone of the human,
Giacometti-wrapped in non-erasure, restarts and retreats?

❖

Aleister Crowley and, later, Kenneth Grant, sought to hang the sexual act with cocoons of alien grandeur, as if the act provides magical access to extra-terrestrial worlds. Before we dismiss their fractal claims, we must spend more time running our fingers over the runic engravings on the inner side of the gold and leaden gate that occasionally opens just a crack in orgasm.

❖

Pregnant stone forever dwelling in its still birth.

Maen ar ya. The rock of yes.

❖

9:50 AM, 1 June. I'm out in the world, placed in a Methodist Hospital basket, on a ledge in the Dordogne, curled up in a Boschian strawberry. Birth is ramose, branching through the caverns of the self, diapered and free, foaming genitalia as well as ascendant Venus, perpetually puckered up inside for that first nipple of light.

❖

The maggot in every artist's craw is his ensign of life.

❖

And the nude with little drawers?
To pull out the breast drawer and, as a child,
fondle the contents. To push back the navel drawer,
the smallest of all, in which there is only room for
the tiniest of ivory elephants. Then to pull out the vagina
   drawer
and, as a child, marvel at the phallic extension.
To place one's child heart in this drawer and, pushing it back
   into forever,
release one's fate from any indebtedness to the order men
   have made.

        Dalí as Christ,
        surrounded by mocking tourists.

           ❖

Out our bedroom window across the neighbors' car park backyard through black walnut trees into two yellow can't-see-through windows. Nothing moves, moves me deeply. Nothing happens in the yellow. I want to see. I want a shadow play to hammer in, the origin of the race. Two yellow windows 30 yards away. They hang there, twins of nothing.

           ❖

Conditioned over ice ages, man as a refrigerated creature. He waits for the door to swing—for God to grasp *him*. Should an apocalypse occur, surely the one plucked forth would only experience the culinary fate that he has, when free to, meted out to others.

❖

Sheela-na-gig, the witch in the wall—she takes off! and like a falcon returns, fence-sitting hag, the *hagazussa*, bridging culture and wilderness: the mind in paradox, holding against dualistic split-offs. Sheela gapes, Sheela shows through, the back wall void shows through her cunt. I am one with her because, deeply, I am a zero, a zero that counts o o o o o o all the way back to the om-matriculated other.

❖

Through the glass wall of Lisita restaurant, Nîmes, November 1999, late evening:

in light rain, next to a flock of leaves by-passed by the mistral, an old man lets his little black dog pee, reluctantly pulling on the thin leash—

to remain within the winding paths of the task, or risk emergence from a labyrinth that has confounded but also provided refuge…

observing and reflecting (no right no wrong), a way to travel and feel ok about dining within the shadow gore of the amphiteatre.

[for Gustaf Sobin]

❖

So now you awake, the labyrinth nearly traversed, stunned by the silence above. Spikes jagging into your tunnel would be one response—but silence? An ennui emits fumes that begin to pervade what must now be thought of as your terminal lair. And here too the figure breaks down, for you are not a mole, even if there are subterranean switchbacks in your way of working, deaf to the arpeggios springing from the ballroom. Or are you some hybrid half-man half-mole? In the hand lamp illumination of a Cro-Magnon wall, an understandable glyph.

❖

Again the tombstones break from their huddle and line up against life.

❖

People of all races in McDonald's, devouring rain forests a football field a second.
Polytheism turns out to be contingent upon the earth's fertile perpetuity.
The gods are not dead—they are, as is the earth, mortal.
An era called: the death of eternity.

❖

First trip to Kyoto, January 1962; having pulled away from the train station, our small taxi passed through a thick snowfall alongside a canal. Snowflakes seen against bar and club variegated neon: cherry blossom ghosts.
It was here, at this moment, I began my own transformation.

Each stands alone on the heart of the earth
transfixed by a ray of sunlight:
all at once

      evening.

          [Quasimodo]

❖

In the beginning was touch, walls everywhere, signed by finger
or palm. Hand negative, color radiating out, hand-embedded wall
turned altar, negative hand. "The Spaniards would cut an Indian's
hands off and leave them dangling by a shred of skin and they would
send him on saying 'Go now, spread the news to your chiefs.'"
Among such spirit hands, I wander today, my hands swinging, hor-
ror mementos, at my side. This hand as an outline of Hispaniola, on
which I locate My Lai.

❖

Medusa must have had a headful of eggs to hatch all those snakes.
Or one big egg, a brain egg, a mental source of life, from which
snakes proliferated.

    Before Medusa: a Cro-Magnon child's terror—at seeing not only
its hunter mother's bloody hands but also her bloody vagina—dis-
places upward, over centuries, to become a snake-wreathed
slaughterface, impacted with holy dread. As if the gate of life were
revealed to contain a carnivorous mouth.

❖

An unmade bed with moist trails of the unmaking. Signs of caravans, of white dunes and sheet lightning. Silo piles, troughed veins in bunched-up folds. Cloud-like quilt swoops, lip-like pleats. Shadowed calms. Orchid-gesturing bends. . .

❖

To write in accordance with what I know is a dead end. I must do the contrary thing: write in accordance with what I seek to know, and intuit that in the crack between knowing and not knowing there is not merely destruction but vision.

❖

The tawny, female form inside the outline of Lascaux's "Chinese horse" is in profile, headless, and pregnant, her paws, or breasts, falling forward. Most interesting: the space between her tawny mass and the outlined belly and legs of the horse that, from this perspective, is a kind of womb for her, for she *is* somewhat foetal. The revelation of the interior of an animal's body appears to be that it contains a human body. Further, that the earth is to strip itself of its animal garments and reveal itself as human. The extinct and endangered confirm that this is exactly what has happened.

❖

Nancy Spero worked herself to life,

churning through the mayhem done to women is
the self-possessed

integrity of Lesbos, without
patriarchal lesions, ties, women in love with

feminine dynamics, the dildos are aswim
in the Dionysus,

the male is a lake of bathing female serpents.

The delectable atmosphere of *A Midsummer Night's Dream*, nature
as fairy-flitted paradise, strands of a shamanistic world in which
spirits communicate. I adore the tree bed in which Titania and
Bottom make love, the bottomless dream in which hybrids mingle
with fairy queens. There is something of *Midsummer* in our life
and love, a sensual, orgasmic mix. I love you so much at 64. Memo-
rial Day: black kids from next door whiz down the sidewalk in carts
and on bikes. We just shared a Veuve Clicquot Rosé, with a few
ounces of caviar, and some canapés you invented: slices of smoked
salmon on tiny crusts smeared with caper red onion butter. A
Ulyssean homecoming every time I step out of the shower.

❖

The Kroger shopper emerges from no Christ cave, but from vegetable and coal, from the meager lore of meat. She is padded, added up, anxious, having passed by *The Star* and *The National Enquirer*. I stand in line, reading myself, the prices, the environment, the shopper. What she has in her cart is a rainbow bucket. I see my cart as the skinned Brazilian trees become charcoal become pig iron used in its steel.

I met a man who told me everything about a man. As he spoke, I wandered ebony corridors, obsidian shafts. His fingers were stained with breasts. He claimed that he issued from everyone and that the Kennedy assassination was the gateway to Atlantis. Oh no you don't, I said, as he gripped the right wing of my girdle, I'm not your toucan, not your marble.

The man who told me everything about a man was windy, empty clothes, a meaty ramrod with sucking porticos. He told me everything is what a man thinks he is. He said that man is a projective demon, whose tendrils shoot their foragings back into the bottomless need to be his own mother.

On Atlantis, he continued, there were no men. Kennedy was preparing to reveal this. Men are post-Atlantean; that is, they only, and vaguely, remember a time. . . a time when. . .

man was an egg dipped in blood,

man was a Sunday outing.

The pickled meow of silence.

❖

~~The river's tent is broken~~
The quiver's bent is oaken:
no way to be more impotent than Eliot.
Although, as upper crust, he can fish with his anus
and coalesce a static yes to
the repressed who teach.
Not that all men must be virile,
it's simply time to lift the Tiresias helmet-mask from Vivian,
to offer her what her soul requires:
the link between the dull roots of modernism and
the confessional pyre.

❖

Imagination, a horse enwebbed in a sea wall of moving clouds—
her hoofs fleck forth embers the mind rerolls, as if between thumb
and whorefinger, loving the slippage as it loves the trenchancy of
the abyssal pour.

❖

Freeing the moment from the hour, your face,
a raindrop in thunder's waste immensity.

❖

All night long
I was an Argiope
as I slept,
laying out draglines, sifting
visual seam for word spore, dragonizing
my agon, working
star wreathes into phrase fairs, excreting
sermon fuel, thread coals,
a shadow self in shaman sores. . .

The queen's pedipalp tapped my shoulder,
plumbed my marrow flora.
                              "Come,
let us irritate the vessels of the earth.
They shall distill strange wine."

Jackson Pollock reclaimed the Aurignacian floor. His next move
might have been to extend the floor to the walls and then move
onto the ceiling, an entire interior turned into a subjectile. Jack the
Whipper. Sawfish dancer from the Torres Straits: "With your strong
stick, scar the ground! As you stab and score, stoop and bow your
head!" Sekhmet's sistrum strings, cat gut and caul. Line as acro-
batic anabasis. The wall ballet at Pech Merle: under exposure of a
mountain showing through a bison showing through a deer.

Dickinson on the cupules gouged in a burial slab at La Ferrassie:

> A Dimple in the Tomb
> Makes that ferocious Room
> A Home—

❖

The lack of a Sisyphus load
drives me horizontal.
I wander, accidental acolyte,
the San Cristobal de las Casas zócalo,
weighing the USA-shadowed blocks,
the timidity of the pizza.
Is my lack a new load?
Could be,   white spectre that I am
could be,   white spectre of I am

The work is self-
indented meaning in a world that denies worlds.

I stand within I, as in shuttle exhaust,
an atom in the fulgurating lift off.

❖

The fuchsia slowly turns and bakes on our front porch, yellowish green if we don't water it.

Bobbing Chinese lanterns, canopied round tree houses for elves, tiny cistern hide-outs, "Sigmund's Hideaways." Bells continuing to proliferate could have been cast by Bosch. Magenta, mallow tinkle homes. Fairies must have originated in fuchsia tang.

❖

Amazing to be this bipedal juggernaut
in Frankenstein to the lightning of the shamans.

❖

The spider is the self, weaving coherently if erratically a labyrinthine over and under world at whose center she waits for males of every stripe: shaman, Theseus, Fulcanelli, the troubadour copulating with the fantasy of his singing. Self's filigree is entangled with its huntress and her husks. All serve death's deepening.

❖

Abandon Here all ye who enter Hope.

❖

Corman:	Hamill:
wild seas (ya to Sado shoring up the great star stream	High over wild seas, surrounding Sado Island: the river of heaven
summer grass warriors dreams ruins	Summer grasses: all that remains of great soldiers' imperial dreams
cruel! under the helmet cricket	Ungraciously, under a great soldier's empty helmet, a cricket sings
quiet into rock absorbing cicada sounds	Lonely silence, a single cicada's cry sinking into stone

Two American poets translating haiku by Bashō. Corman: language as enactment, the reader interprets. Hamill: language as interpretation, the reader abandoned. Corman is deft where Hamill is pleonastic and inaccurate (crickets don't sing; cicadas don't cry). In a haiku-like poem of his own, Corman writes:

> The cicada
> singing isn't;
> that sound's its life.

❖

My gate is ired by Artaud, austered by Vallejo,
laminariaed by Césaire. Gate guards
complexing the vulnerability of vision.

My work is my shrine. I ask my guards to process
anyone seeking to enter.
If you want into my penetralia,

pass through the translations.
Then you will see to what
my own work is and is not beholden.

I decided that I knew no more than 1 percent of existence. I held this
percent, a penny, in my hand and let it fall into the abyss of what I
did not know. It struck Lascaux. Am I now entitled to claim a sec-
ond penny? Or would it be more honest to walk on, lost, having cre-
ated, in effect, no sound to mask my encyclopedic ignorance?

July cloudburst, luciflailing maples,
sun-burnt top leaves shredding
patter gnomes, pupa ghosts, fairies
    in freckled pounce

To be in the rush of the core, to feel
    the rout side.

❖

Peter Beard juxtaposes dead African animals with celebrities and fashion models. I doubt that he intends a metaphor, but what bawls out at me from these collages is: fashion and celebrity = dead animals. Not "pheasant under glass" but nude model under poached elephant tusk. Marginal graffiti buzzing blow-ups of the unending destruction of African wildlife. And how does one read Beard himself posed halfway out of a dead crocodile's jaws, scribbling in a notebook? The final grounding of Jonah's emergence? Rimbaud sat Beauty on his lap and found her peter bearded. Karen Blixen juxtaposed with a flayed leopard; Francis Bacon's whipped-cream flesh, with bulbous African bellies. We'll begin dinner with a giraffe foetus, and follow with caviar, driftwood, and legs.

❖

Derrida like a virus in Artaud's texts, autocatalytically spreading here and there. After two hours, the standing-room-only audience wandered out of the MOMA auditorium. Only a handful, I'm convinced, understood anything. But come they did, to view the appearance of a "holy man" on Hotel Artaud's shit-smeared balcony.

❖

The poem, a tumor-entangled, umbilical sight-line.

❖

Beyond the shadow, doubt. Without a shadow, no doubt. Without doubt, we are the greatest. We are the greatest shadow of doubt. Without the great test of doubt, we are the shadow.

Brattleboro VT: shiny scarlet ivy with dark red Methodist brick showing through. In Edvard Munch's *La Vigne vierge*, a spooked man flees a mansion whose walls are covered with tentacular red magma. Men should praise woman's liminal, bronze red lake, ever molting, ever still.

❖

When dream crossed into closed-eye vision, when phosphene and phantom merged, image was cocked, ready from the fingers to fire, ready on the fingers, as fire, as suns, zigzags, spirals, along with celestial drapery, shredded in the eyeball crucible. Dream was tricked forth from its lair, parasympathetically moved to a human edge, so that eye writing is first—dot dot dot dot dot dot dot dot dot SQUARE! Point into uncial, hooking lines closing in upon themselves as part of the drama of image fauna being separated out of humankind. Wavering dream forms of mist and ice. Faceted crystalline beast head buried in Beauty.

❖

In the not-too-distant future, civilization will consist of Disney-like archipelagos populated by entertainers, tourists, and refugees.

It is said that by 2005 there will be more living on earth than the total sum of those who have lived (the dead). Could these possibly break through the floor of consciousness yielding the abyss of the unconscious, giving them direct access to the living?

Such archipelagos will be dominated by scenarios and tableaux of ages past. A Noh-like atmosphere: the unappeased dead seeking to realize their fate in the consciousness of the living.

At such a time, it may become possible to see into death.

Whitman's hand lathered with Civil War. Dickinson void of slavery, prostitution, hell. They signal to us, these two most moving pyres. Contraries transforming circumference into adhesive love. Such has never seemed more important to imagination than now as the millennium bulges in its sty.

[Ypsilanti, 1986–2000]

NOTES

Concerning Gnomes and Trolls: The quotation, from a preliminary report on Buchenwald, April 1945, is to be found in Robert H. Abzug's *Inside the Vicious Heart: Americans and the Liberation of Nazi Concentration Camps* (New York: Oxford University Press, 1987), p. 56.

Song: Photographs of the napalmed Vietnamese girls can be found in *Caterpillar #3/4*. Robert Duncan addresses these faces in his variations on Robert Southwell's "Burning Babe," part of "A Seventeenth Century Suite," in *Ground Work: Before the War* (New York: New Directions, 1984).

Across the Bering Strait: Photos of Mary Ann Unger's sculptural installation "Across the Bering Strait," at the Trans Hudson Gallery, Jersey City, 1994, are in *Sulfur #40* (with an essay on Unger by Carla Harryman); other photos of this material are in *Mary Ann Unger*, a catalogue produced for the Trans Hudson Gallery and New Jersey State Museum shows in 1997.

Blue Zone: Ann Mikolowski (1940–1999) was a central figure in Detroit's Cass Corridor art movement. Her work ranges from expansive, open vistas of water and sky, to tiny, realistic portraits of artists and friends. Along with her husband, Ken, she was editor, publisher, and printer of the Alternative Press broadsides and postcards for over thirty years. She provided cover art for such magazines as *Hanging Loose* (see #75 in particular, with six color reproductions of her sky- and landscapes, along with a tribute to her by Donna Brook), *Dispatch*, *Moving Out*, and *New American Writing*. Her paintings appeared on the covers of books by such writers as Helen Adam, Robert Creeley, Faye Kicknosway, William Stafford, and, most recently, Adrienne Rich.

Shopping: The quotation is from Tillie Olson's poem "I Want You Women Up North to Know," published in 1934.

Sparks We Trail: A reproduction of the Mu-ch'i "Persimmons" serves as the frontispiece to Daisetz Suzuki's *Zen and Japanese Culture* (New York: Pantheon, 1959).

The Hybrid Is the Engine of Anima Display: This engraving is extremely difficult to "read," and even though I have seen it twice in the "sanctuary" of Les Trois Frères, like others I have studied it mainly on the basis of the Abbé Henri Breuil's drawings. The best source for his drawings of the engraved panels in Les Trois Frères is *Les Cavernes du volp* (Paris: Arts et métiers graphiques, 1958).

Craniologue: Steven Stanley discusses his ideas about what triggered the expansion of continental ice sheets (the rising of the Isthmus of Panama around three million years ago, which changed the circulation patterns within the earth's great oceans, leaving the Arctic Ocean without a heat supply) in *Children of the Ice Age* (New York: Freeman & Co., 1998), Chapter 7.

Cemeteries of Paradise: Henry Miller's stirring evocation of the prehistoric Dordogne occurs in his book on Greece, *The Colossus of Maroussi* (New York: New Directions, 1958), pp. 4–5. Miller seems to have prepared for his trip to Greece by visiting the Dordogne, and seems to have known about the caves. In the evocation itself there is no evidence that he visited any.

A dream of 16 February 2000, enacting the devolution of Charles Olson, may have cleared the way for this poem as well as my definition of one phase of my work as a poet ("I hunt inside stone") set against the last line of "The Kingfishers."

Near a beach I discovered mole hills between kennels or chicken coops. A farmer said he'd turn his dogs on them. I watched furious fighting inside a shed, lots of mole-pups being spit out. Worried that Caryl would not know where to find me, I started walking a path to suddenly find myself in a crowd where I heard that Charles Olson, now out on the road with a small child, wandering and giving lectures for food, for some eighty days, was to arrive. I was shown photos of Robert Kelly with a young black woman and other strangers. Then I was in a house with people who had studied Olson, including an attractive Irish woman who had a small tansu set into the floor. She said it contained Olson texts and could not be opened until he arrived. The excitement was mounting—Olson enthusiasts seemed to be everywhere. I was now in a spacious cave and heard the approach of what I took to be Olson and his retinue—there he was, seven feet tall, shaggy white hair, thin neck, large block-like skeletal head, hunched over, climbing through the air. I went up to him, took his huge hand. He looked at me curiously, then boomed: "How are your caves coming along?" I started to describe the completion of *Juniper Fuse*, but he interrupted: "The music, how about the music?" Before I could respond, he was past me. I was surrounded by hip-looking men in sunglasses who I figured were Olson aviators. It was a joyous occasion—then it hit me: how could he be here? He died in 1970! Larry Goodell then piped up: "That's the majesty of it!" I was now caught up in another crowd, and being shown a map of the Pech Merle cave with certain areas marked which I understood Olson had explored. "Olson is coming!" I heard. "What?" I said, "I just saw him!" "No, he's coming now," voices clamored, and a strange creature rounded a cave bend, a leg-like head with one huge eye, stick-like body, insect legs. "No, this is not Olson—I JUST SAW OLSON!" I shouted. There was intense conversation about what was referred to as a "restoration." New people appeared, shouting that Olson was on his way! An even stranger apparition appeared, more insectile, arachnoid, long extending legs front and back, its head—a compact lavender mass—under its body. I worked my way under as the creature ambled along, yelling "What happened to you?" I got my hands around the jewel-like head and wrenched it free, at which moment an agonized voice cried: "*I couldn't get the whole Theolonius!*" What was left disappeared among the mass of people thronging the cave.

121

Erratics: I became aware of the noun "erratic"—a rock or boulder transported from its original resting place, especially by ice—in 1999, in an article by Andrew Schelling on Philip Whalen. Soon after, while organizing literary archival materials, I discovered some fifteen hundred pages of worksheets from the late 1980s and early 1990s with material that had not been worked up for publication. Some drafts had been revised again and again, then abandoned; others were beginnings that, appearing to lead nowhere, had been set aside and forgotten. I would occasionally find a line or a patch of writing that was effective, so I set these pages aside. All of this material was problematic, as it was buried in surrounding material that no longer interested me. Finally, I typed up on separate pages the lines I wanted to do something with.

One morning it occurred to me that these fragments could be thought of as erratics, vagabonds that had wandered from their original contexts. In their own way, they were like rocks found in a field whose original resting places were obscure. At this point I had several hundred "erratics," to which I added another hundred from more recent worksheets. As I moved them around, many ceased to hold up, and as I winnowed, I realized that since all had been removed from their original locations a chronological presentation made no sense. A thematic presentation was also unsatisfactory, as the hundred or so "erratics" consisted of aphorisms (at several points during the editing process I revisited Wallace Stevens' "Adagia"), sightings on literature and politics, short poems without titles, prose fragments, dreams, and statements—only a few of which directly related to one another.

Given the definition of the word "erratic," I decided that a chance order might be appropriate. I typed all of the first lines on slips of paper and dropped them into our rotating lettuce-dryer. After it was spun, Caryl picked the slips out of the basket without looking and then placed them on my desk in the order she had picked them. Certain juxtapositions revealed correspondences between pieces that I had not detected. I retyped the manuscript in this new and almost final order, again taking out some pieces that now did not seem to belong, while adjusting words and phrases in others.

The result is a constellation of seventy-six pieces, an erratic company that makes up an image of what concerns me about life at large. I'd like to think that each entry is a rock, integral and enigmatic, a weight as well as a gate, and that each holds its own in the same spirit that a rock on the ground occupies and possesses its own space.

[September 2001]

CLAYTON ESHLEMAN was born in Indianapolis, Indiana, in 1935. The author of more than twenty books, including twelve collections of poetry published by Black Sparrow Press, he is the recipient of the National Book Award, a Guggenheim Fellowship, several fellowships from the National Endowment for the Arts and the National Endowment for the Humanities, and the Landon Translation Prize from the Academy of American Poets. He is also a prolific and masterly translator, especially from the Spanish of Neruda and Vallejo and the French of Artaud and Césaire. In 2003, Wesleyan University Press published Eshleman's *Juniper Fuse: Upper Paleolithic Imagination and the Construction of the Underworld*, the fruit of a thirty-year investigation into the origins of image-making and poetry via the painted caves of southwestern France. A professor emeritus of English at Eastern Michigan University, he lives in Ypsilanti with his wife, Caryl.